# Management Turnover, Regulatory Oversight, and Performance:

# Evidence From Community Banks

Ajay A. Palvia

*Office of the Comptroller of Currency*

OCC Economics Working Paper 2008-1

Version Date: April 29, 2010

Keywords: executive turnover, regulatory oversight, performance, corporate governance JEL Classifications: G30, G28, G31.

The views expressed in this paper are those of the author alone and do not necessarily reflect the views of the Office of the Comptroller of the Currency or the U.S. Department of the Treasury. Please address correspondence to the author at Office of the Comptroller of the Currency, 250 E St. SW, Washington, DC 20219. The author also can be reached via e-mail at ajay.palvia@occ.treas.gov.

The author would like to thank Irina Barakova, Michael Carhill, Fred Finke, Yaniv Grinstein, Mark Levonian, Min Qi, Gary Whalen, Peihwang Wei, Office of the Comptroller of Currency seminar participants, International Conference on Business and Finance participants, and Southwestern Finance Association conference participants. The author takes responsibility for any errors.

**Management Turnover, Regulatory Oversight, and
Performance: Evidence From Community Banks**

**Ajay A. Palvia**

April 29, 2010

**Abstract:** This paper exploits a unique panel of U.S. community banks to re-examine the role of regulatory oversight in disciplining bank management and to consider the effect of such regulatory-linked disciplinary actions on subsequent bank performance. The results indicate that both weak bank performance and poor regulatory evaluations are associated with increased executive turnover. Furthermore, the relationship between poor regulatory evaluations and turnover persists after controlling for performance. Finally, executive turnover linked to poor regulatory evaluations is found to be positively related to future performance. Overall, the findings are consistent with the explanation that regulatory oversight can lead to improved bank governance.

# I. Introduction

Bank shareholders, like shareholders of unregulated firms, delegate the monitoring of top management to company boards of directors. Unlike, other firms, however, banks are also subject to regulatory monitoring, which has the potential to improve oversight by providing bank boards with additional information or by prodding bank boards to more dutifully consider existing information. To the extent regulatory oversight helps, or forces, bank boards to discipline ineffective management, it has the potential to improve bank governance.[1]

Regulatory monitoring of banks largely consists of rating banks, communicating the rationale behind the ratings to banks, and initiating either formal or informal actions when important deficiencies in banks are found.[2] If regulatory monitoring uncovers information signifying ineffective or inept management, it may lead to the replacement of senior management. This paper considers the role of regulatory monitoring in promoting better bank governance. In particular, it examines whether regulatory evaluations influence top management turnover and whether such regulatory-induced turnover is associated with better subsequent performance.

Numerous past instances of top management replacement suggest that regulatory monitoring can play a disciplinary role in banks. For example, an Office of the Comptroller of the Currency (OCC) bank examination found poor internal controls at a community bank in 2001; soon thereafter, the bank's CEO was fired by its board (OCC, 2002). In more recent cases, Coast Bank of Florida and Westsound Bank, both facing pressure from investigations

---

[1] Because bank assets tend to be opaque (Iannotta, 2004; Morgan, 2002), regulatory monitoring of banking firms may be especially beneficial.

[2] Typical informal actions include commitment letters, memorandums of understanding, and safety and soundness plans and are not publicly disclosed. Formal actions are generally more severe and publicly disclosed. The U.S. bank regulatory system is described further in the next section.

by bank regulators for loan fraud, announced the resignations of their CEOs (Frater and Pollick, 2007; Gardner, 2008). These actions support the view that regulatory oversight, at least in some cases, is associated with turnover of ineffective or inept bank management. This paper explores whether the association between regulatory oversight and top management dismissals is systematic. Further, it examines whether regulatory-linked turnover of top management improves bank performance.

Overall, this paper finds that, consistent with past studies of large, publicly traded firms, poorly performing community banks are more likely to have top management turnover. It also finds that greater regulatory pressure, as indicated by recent regulatory examinations, weak regulatory ratings, and recent rating downgrades, is associated with more executive turnover after controlling for bank performance. Finally, turnover linked to regulatory monitoring is significantly, positively related to future profitability. Taken as a whole, the evidence suggests that regulatory oversight improves bank discipline and can help to improve bank performance and, implicitly, bank governance.

A key distinguishing feature of this study is a unique dataset of about 3,000 community banks and over 74,000 observations spanning a decade.[3] The large sample and the large number of years allow for significant variation in both management turnover and bank financial performance. The study focuses on community banks—which tend to be small, geographically concentrated, and privately held—for two reasons.[4] First, neither the effect of performance on turnover nor the impact of regulatory monitoring on turnover is well

---

[3] The dataset is based on executive turnover data from 1985 to 1994 for nationally chartered U.S. banks. Although the full dataset contains over 74,000 bank-quarter observations, some of the multivariate tests utilize a somewhat reduced observation set because of econometric issues; these issues are discussed later in the paper.

[4] While there is no formal definition of "community banks," such banks generally have very small branch networks and low levels of assets; consistent with available data, this paper defines community banks as banks with assets of $100 million or less.

4

understood for smaller or private banks. Additionally, because market and board oversight may not be as strong for community banks and if managerial replacements induced by regulatory monitoring lead to improvements in bank governance, the improvements should be easier to identify in community banks relative to larger, publicly traded banks.

A large number of studies have examined the relationship between past stock performance and CEO turnover and usually found a negative relationship.[5] The benefits of such turnover on subsequent performance, and implicitly on bank governance, are not as clear, however. The existing literature does document a positive relationship between turnover of poorly performing management and subsequent performance (Denis and Denis, 1995; Hotchkiss, 1995; Khorana, 2001). These studies suggest that managerial discipline linked to traditional monitoring by boards can improve performance. In contrast, the impact of management turnover on performance arising from nontraditional monitoring mechanisms, such as regulatory oversight, is less clear. This is the first study, to my knowledge, to explore the performance impact of management turnover arising from such nontraditional monitoring mechanisms. In providing evidence that management turnover linked to regulatory monitoring is associated with improved bank performance, this paper suggests that regulatory monitoring of bank management leads to better bank governance and is not entirely driven by compliance with regulation.

In the next section, I describe the key aspects of the regulatory examination process of banks and consider its role in bank governance. The data are described in section III. In sections IV and V, I present the empirical results and draw some conclusions.

---

[5] Brickley (2003) provides a good review of this literature.

## II. Regulatory Oversight, Bank Examinations, and Bank Governance

The U.S. bank regulatory system is complex and composed of both state and federal regulators. Banks with state banking charters are overseen jointly by their state regulatory agency and by either the Federal Reserve or the Federal Deposit Insurance Corporation (FDIC). The OCC oversees nationally chartered banks.[6] Regardless of regulatory agency, federal regulators examine vast amounts of information during the examination process and a major product of the examination process is a regulatory rating of a bank's overall condition, commonly referred to as a CAMELS rating. It is used by all the three federal banking regulators.

The CAMELS rating is an overall assessment of a bank based on six individual ratings; the word CAMELS is an acronym for these individual elements of regulatory assessment (capital adequacy, asset quality, management, earnings, liquidity, and sensitivity to market risk).[7] The overall CAMELS rating and each individual component rating are private and confidential. Regulatory agencies do not release ratings; even historical CAMELS ratings or ratings of banks no longer in existence are not released.

All individual component ratings as well as the overall ratings are coded on a scale of 1 to 5 with "1" being best (no regulatory concern) and "5" being worst (very serious regulatory concerns). Banks with weak CAMEL ratings (generally "3," "4," and "5") tend to be monitored more aggressively by regulators and often are faced with informal and

---

[6] For more details on the organization of the banking system, see Fabozzi et al. (2002), chapter 3. For information on banking laws and regulations, see www.fdic.gov/regulations/laws.

[7] The last component in the acronym CAMELS, sensitivity to market risk, is a relatively new feature and was introduced in 1997. Because the period of study in this paper precedes 1997, the rest of this paper will refer only to CAMEL.

sometimes formal regulatory actions. Thus, weaker ratings should be associated with greater regulatory pressure.

Although many of the individual components of CAMEL are likely to be correlated, they are not identical. This paper's focus is on the management ratings. According to the OCC definition, regulatory management ratings are based on "a) technical competence, leadership, and administration ability, b) compliance with banking regulations and statutes, c) ability to plan and respond to changing circumstances, d) adequacy of and compliance with internal policies, e) depth and succession, f) tendencies toward self-dealing, g) demonstrated willingness to serve the legitimate banking needs of the community."

Although much of the information in the CAMEL or management component ratings can be deduced from publicly available financial information, an increasing number of studies indicate that the regulatory information in these ratings cannot be fully explained by publicly available information (DeYoung et al., 2001; Peek et al., 1998). Given that most of the guidelines upon which the management regulatory rating is based are consistent with good corporate governance, regulatory actions based on private information contained in these ratings could potentially help improve the governance of banks.

Previous evidence implies that the bank examination process may lead to improved bank governance in terms of forcing banks to more fully report loan losses (Dahl et al., 1998; Gunther and Moore, 2003). Although several studies have also implied that regulatory oversight drives management turnover in banks (Houston and James, 1993; Prowse, 1995; Webb, 2008), results from these studies may not necessarily indicate that such oversight is beneficial. For example, if the turnover attributable to regulatory pressure is primarily a result of compliance issues and not because of ineffective or inept management, then regulatory-linked replacement of top management may not improve governance. Furthermore, if regulatory-linked managerial discipline simply replaces the disciplinary role of boards (Cook et al., 2004), regulatory oversight of bank management may not improve bank governance.

To address the question of whether regulatory oversight is beneficial in improving bank governance, this paper focuses on community banks, where the potential benefits of regulatory oversight should be the greatest. Detailed governance data on these banks, however, are not available to directly address this question. Fortunately, because improved governance is generally associated with better performance, improved governance owing to regulatory oversight can be inferred if the management turnover linked to this oversight is also related to better subsequent performance. By examining whether bank regulatory oversight is associated with turnover and then exploring whether turnover linked to regulatory oversight is related to improved performance, this paper explores whether regulatory monitoring of bank management can lead to improved bank governance.

## III. Data

All financial data are based on call report data, which is publicly available for all U.S. banks. Private regulatory variables are obtained from the OCC. Because regulatory data are only available for national banks, the sample is restricted to these banks. Regulatory ratings of bank management are used, rather than information regarding the issuance of formal actions. Regulatory ratings implicitly factor in both formal and informal actions and also incorporate the effects of communication between regulators and bank boards that do not culminate in a specific formal or informal action. Accordingly, the use of regulatory ratings allows for a more comprehensive measure of regulatory oversight than indicators of whether a bank is facing an explicit enforcement action.

The key data on executive turnover are only available for community banks, defined as banks having assets of up to $100 million, between 1984 and 1994.[8] Additionally, the sample is restricted to banks that are not part of a multibank holding company (MBHC) for two reasons. First, this reduces the likelihood that banks in the sample are indirectly influenced by market pressures of large organizations through an affiliation with a MBHC. Secondly, bank management may have multiple roles within a holding company or may be influenced by the holding company board. Because the data do not allow the identification of roles of senior bank management or the makeup of boards within the subsidiaries of a holding company and its parent organization, the role of regulatory ratings of bank management is more difficult to interpret in these types of organizations. The elimination of banks affiliated with MBHCs reduces the sample further by about 25 percent. Because of the data restrictions, the results of the paper will apply to community banks that are not part of MBHCs and may not necessarily apply to larger banks or banks that are part of larger banking organizations. Despite these data restrictions, the sample contains an overwhelming majority of national banks and the results apply to a broader number of banks and bank classes than previous studies focusing on large, publicly traded banks.[9]

---

[8] The executive turnover variable was only required to be reported for banks filling out a Federal Financial Institutions Examination Council (FFIEC) 034 reporting form. This excludes banks with assets of $100 million or more and was only available between 1984 and 1994.

[9] Although virtually all banks in the sample are private, the data do not allow for the identification of those few that are not. Given the very small number of publicly traded banks in general, and even smaller number of small publicly traded banks, the number of publicly traded banks in this sample is likely to be inconsequential.

For the most part, banks in the sample are included for all time periods in which data are available.[10] Thus the dataset consists of an unbalanced panel, in which banks remain in the sample for varying number of years during the observation period (as new banks form and existing banks are acquired or exit for other reasons). The data are not restricted to banks remaining in the sample over the entire period, because this would have greatly reduced the sample size and would lead to considerable survivorship bias. All financial variables are winsorized, at the bottom 1-percent and top 1-percent levels to minimize the effect of outliers. After creating lagged values of key variables, the final dataset consists of about 3,000 banks and over 74,000 bank-quarter observations during the 10-year period between 1985 and 1994.[11]

*a) Variables*

The key variable in the analysis indicates whether a change in senior executive officer occurred during the quarter (EXTURN). A senior executive officer is defined as any one of the top three officers in the bank; these officers, regardless of their official titles, perform the functions of a chief executive officer, president, or senior lending officer. A change can occur for any reason, including resignation, retirement, death, or demotion (to a non-senior officer).

---

[10] An exception to this is banks that failed during the sample period. Observations from banks that failed for the one-year period immediately preceding failure are excluded, because financial data so close to failure may not be reliable. This reduces the sample size by about 1 percent. Additional tests, not reported, indicate the results are not affected by this exclusion.

[11] There about 3,000 total banks in the sample over the entire sample. Because of bank acquisitions, bank failures, and newly chartered banks, the actual number of observations at any given point ranges from about 1,400 to about 2,300.

For banks with fewer than three senior officers, an additional officer being hired to a senior role is also counted as a change.[12]

Three variables are used to measure regulatory monitoring of banks. The first of these is the regulatory rating for management (MANRAT); like CAMEL ratings, MANRAT ranges from "1" (best) to "5" (worst). Secondly, I include the change in the management rating during the quarter. Positive values of the change in rating variable (CHANGERAT) indicate regulatory downgrades. I use the change in the rating, rather than a dummy indicating a downgrade, to allow for the fact that downgrades of more than one notch may have a different impact relative to downgrades of only one notch.[13] The variables MANRAT and CHANGERAT capture different dimensions of regulatory oversight. While MANRAT captures the current regulatory opinion of bank management (and implicitly the effect of past downgrades), CHANGERAT captures a recent change in regulatory opinion of bank management. All else being equal, we should expect poorly rated bank management and management whose ratings have been recently downgraded to be associated greater regulatory pressure on management and thus higher turnover. The third regulatory oversight variable included is a dummy indicating whether an exam was conducted in the last 18 months (EXAMINED). Typically, banks exams are conducted every 12–18 months; sometimes, banks are not examined for years. Faced with limited resources, regulators typically prioritize examinations to focus on banks with suspected problems. The inclusion of EXAMINED acknowledges that banks may not always be examined with equal regularity and a decision by

---

[12] The turnover variable is derived from a call report variable indicating whether a change in senior officers has occurred in a given quarter. A limitation of this data is that turnover cannot be attributed to a particular senior officer.

[13] In practice, only a small percentage of downgrades (about 10 percent) are associated with changes in the management rating by more than one notch; for robustness, I replace CHANGERAT with a dummy indicating that a downgrade occurred. The results are unchanged.

11

regulators to conduct an exam may itself indicate a lack of regulatory confidence in a bank or its management.

Bank performance is measured by the return on assets (ROA), which is defined as net income to assets. To control for other aspects of bank financial condition, I include measures for financial leverage, liquidity, and credit risk. I proxy for credit risk using the dollar amount of loans more than 90 days past due or under nonaccrual status divided by assets (PDUE90). Liquidity (LIQUID) is proxied by the amount of nonvolatile liabilities scaled by assets.[14] Financial leverage is controlled for using the capital ratio based on Tier-1 capital (CAPRAT).[15] To control for size, I also include the log of total assets (LGASSET).

Lastly, I include controls relating to bank organizational structure and market factors. Given the large dataset of mostly private firms, detailed data regarding organizational, board, and ownership structure are not available. Instead, several other observable characteristics that may cause executive turnover are accounted for. First, I include a dummy indicating whether the bank has acquired another bank during the quarter (ACQUIRE); banks that have acquired other banks are more likely to have redundant management and are more likely to have higher executive turnover.[16] Additionally, because newer banks are likely to have less experienced management, management turnover could be different for these banks. To control for this, I include a dummy indicating that the bank is a de novo bank (DENOVO); I define "de novo" as being chartered within the last five years.

---

[14] Volatile liabilities are defined as including large certificates of deposit, federal funds purchases, demand notes issued to the U.S. Treasury, foreign office deposits, and adjusted trading liabilities.

[15] The Tier-1 capital ratio is defined as: (Tier-1 Capital) / (Average Total Assets − Disallowed Intangibles). Tier-1 capital is considered the most reliable and is a key measure of capital used by bank regulators. It generally consists of common stock, irredeemable and noncumulative preferred stock, and retained earnings.

[16] The variable defines an acquisition as an unassisted acquisition (not assisted by the FDIC or other federal agencies in any way).

Although ownership structure of the bank is not available, it is possible to identify when a bank moves from nonaffiliated status to becoming a bank-holding company member, when a bank moves from being affiliated to a holding company to being affiliated with a different holding company, and also when a bank goes from being a member of holding company to being unaffiliated. A measure of change in ownership, OWNCHANGE—indicating any of the above changes, is included in the analysis because these changes may lead to redundant management or reorganizations resulting in executive turnover.[17]

Because executives may leave a bank voluntarily, it would be beneficial to control for other potential causes of executive turnover, such as retirement or accepting employment elsewhere. Unfortunately, no information is available about average executive age or other factors that may affect a decision to retire. A bank executive's decision to accept employment elsewhere, however, is likely to be affected by the number of bank executive positions in the market where the bank operates. To control for voluntary turnover, I include two additional variables. First, I include the percentage of *other* banks in the market (metropolitan statistical area or rural county) experiencing turnover during the quarter (EXTURNMKT). Secondly, the variable BANKSMKT, which indicates the number of banks currently operating in the market, is included.[18] BANKSMKT may also proxy for higher market-level competition;

---

[17] Although banks belonging to multibank holding companies are excluded from the sample, some banks still choose to operate as single-bank holding companies. Ownership structure can change when a bank becomes affiliated as a holding company or when a bank's affiliation to a holding company is ended.

[18] Although the univariate and multivariate tests include only national community banks, all U.S. banks were included in defining BANKSMKT. All banks were included because national banks are likely to face competitive pressures not only from other national banks but also non-national banks.

banks located in markets with greater competition may be more willing to replace poorly performing management.[19]

Finally, executive turnover is likely to depend on executive tenure for multiple reasons. First, relatively new senior executives are less likely to be entrenched and are, therefore, more vulnerable to being disciplined. An additional factor could be that senior management turnover happens in waves. Because our measure of turnover, EXTURN, includes turnover in any of the top three executive positions of a bank, it is possible that turnover in one quarter could be associated with turnover in the following quarter, as subsequent quarters could be associated with different executives. Thus short tenure of top management (TENSHORT) is measured as turnover in the prior quarter and is included in the analysis.

### b) Descriptive Statistics

Summary statistics for all variables are provided in table 1. The mean for the turnover variable, EXTURN, shows that about 8.5 percent of banks had senior executive changes in any given quarter during the observation period. The regulatory variable MANRAT has a mean of 2.33 and a median of 2. This suggests that the majority of banks are rated highly, (i.e., "1" or "2"). The regulatory variable CHANGERAT is reported in table 1 only for observations when a change in a rating has occurred.[20] CHANGERAT, for banks with ratings changes, has a mean of 0.06 and 5th percentile and 95th percentile values of −1 and 2,

---

[19] Market-level data, from which measures such as the Herfindahl index could be computed, are not available during this time period. Because banks in the sample are mostly local community banks, the number of banks in the market may serve as a good proxy for competition in the local metropolitan statistical area or county in which a bank is located.

[20] Because most banks (over 90 percent) are not downgraded or upgraded in any given quarter, presentation of CHANGERAT in this form is helpful in describing the distribution of ratings changes. In all univariate and multivariate tests, CHANGERAT is set to 0 when no rating change occurred in the quarter.

respectively. This suggests that while the overwhelming majority of ratings changes are only one notch up or down, sometimes larger changes do occur. The mean of the last regulatory variable, EXAMINED, is about 88 percent, which indicates that most banks have been examined in the previous 18 months.

The average log assets (LGASSET), measured in thousands of dollars, is 10.48, which implies the average bank size is $35 million during the entire time period. Similarly, the 5th percentile, median, and 95th percentile size is roughly $11 million, $38 million, and $92 million, respectively. Thus, there is a wide range of bank sizes within the sample of community banks. The mean of change in log assets (CHLGASSET) is 0.07 while the 5th percentile and 95th percentile is −0.09 and 0.30, respectively; this indicates that, on average, banks grow from quarter to quarter, but some banks shrink.

The variation in performance (ROA) and financial condition is considerable in the sample. The 5th and 95th percentile ROA is −1.48 percent and 2.02 percent, respectively. Similarly, large ranges between the 5th and 95th percentile values of past-due loans (PDUE), capital ratio (CAPRAT), and liquidity (LIQUID) indicate that other elements of financial condition also vary dramatically across the sample. The 5th percentile to 95th range for PDUE90, CAPRAT, and LIQUID are 0.01 percent, 4.36 percent; 4.98 percent, 15.36 percent; and 70.92 percent, 98.55 percent; respectively.

The mean value for DENOVO indicates that newer (de novo) banks make up about 11.58 percent of the banks in the sample. A very small portion of banks, i.e., about 0.53 percent, acquire (ACQUIRE) other banks in any given quarter and about 1.01 percent of banks have had a change in ownership (OWNCHANGE) in any given quarter. The average and median number of banks in the market (BANKSMKT) in the sample is about 35 and 7, respectively; these numbers suggest that most markets have relatively small numbers of banks but a few very competitive markets lead to a higher overall average market size. Finally, the mean and median percentage of other banks in the market with turnover (EXTURNMKT) is 8.1 percent and 0.0 percent, respectively; thus most markets witness no turnover in other banks, while some witness a relatively large amount.

## III. Empirical Results

To examine how top manager turnover relates to regulatory pressure and performance, I first conduct univariate tests relating managerial turnover to regulatory pressure and performance. Next, the same question is examined through multivariate techniques. Further tests explore the question of whether regulatory-linked managerial turnover is related to future performance.

### a) Univariate Tests: Performance and Regulatory Pressure—the Effect on Turnover

Table 2 divides the sample by time period and by whether executive turnover occurred in the quarter. The first three years of the sample (1986–1988) represent a period immediately following bank deregulation, high levels of competition in the industry, and an increasing number of bank failures; the next three years (1989–1991) are characterized by even more bank failures and the enacting of new, risk-based capital standards to limit risk-taking incentives by bank management. The last few years (1992–1994) are characterized by a more stable banking environment and improved bank profitability.

The results indicate that there are some differences in the performance and regulatory variables over time. Performance (ROA) tends to improve in later time periods relative to the first time period. Ratings downgrades, as indicated by higher values of CHANGERAT, are also somewhat more widespread in the earlier two periods of the sample relative to the latter period. Finally, the percentage of banks examined in the last 18 months (EXAMINED) seems to be somewhat smaller in the earliest period relative to the latter periods. Nevertheless, performance (ROA) is worse, regulatory ratings are worse (higher MANRAT), rating downgrades are more prevalent (higher CHANGERAT), and recent examinations are more likely to have occurred (EXAMINED) for banks when there was executive turnover regardless of time period. The differences between banks with and without executive turnover are statistically significant in every time period of the sample.

The tests described in table 2 indicate that both performance and bank regulatory pressure play a part in bank executive turnover but do not account for these factors simultaneously. To address this issue, additional tests are conducted to examine the simultaneous impact of regulatory monitoring and performance. The results of these tests are shown in table 3. Here, the level of performance (ROA) is divided into quartiles and the regulatory variables are summarized for each of these quartiles separately, for banks that did and did not experience turnover. It can be observed that regulatory pressure is stronger for banks with worse performance, (i.e., worse ratings, greater prevalence of downgrades, and increased likelihood of recent exams). Despite the correlation between performance and greater regulatory pressure, the results clearly indicate that the management ratings tend to be worse, downgrades are more widespread, and recent regulatory examinations are more likely to have occurred for banks with turnover for each quartile of performance. Overall, the results of table 3 are consistent with both performance and regulatory pressure being drivers of executive turnover.

17

## b) Multivariate Tests: Performance and Regulatory Pressure—the Effect on Turnover

While the univariate statistics are clearly consistent with managerial turnover being driven by both performance and regulatory evaluations of bank management, they may not adequately adjust for other aspects of bank financial condition or nonfinancial factors that may influence turnover. If these other factors are really driving executive turnover, then not adequately accounting for them may lead to inaccurate conclusions. To control for these factors, multivariate regressions are conducted, controlling for key financial variables and other controls. A logistic model is employed for these tests as shown in the following equation.

$$
(1) \quad
\begin{aligned}
Log(&\frac{\Pr ob(EXTURN_{i,t}=1)}{1-\Pr ob(EXTURN_{i,t}=1)} = B_0 * MANRAT_{i,t-1} + B_1 * CHANGERAT_{i,t-1} \\
&+ B_2 * EXAMINED_{i,t-1} + B_3 * ROA_{i,t-1} + \sum_{j=4}^{8} B_j * FC_{j;i,t-1} + t - 1 \\
&+ \sum_{j=9}^{14} B_j * NFC_{j;i,t} + TIME_t + BANK_i + \varepsilon_{i,t}
\end{aligned}
$$

In equation (1), FC is a vector of financial controls (PDUE90, CAPRAT, LIQUID, LGASSET, and CHLGASSET). The second vector, NFC, includes the nonfinancial controls (DENOVO, ACQUIRE, OWNCHANGE, TENSHORT, BANKSMT, and EXTURNMKT). To mitigate the effect of other omitted bank variables, I include bank fixed effects. Time dummies are also included to minimize the effect of unobserved macroeconomic or industry factors. In each of these regressions, MANRAT, CHANGERATE, EXAMINED, ROA, and the other financial variables are lagged to minimize potential endogeneity problems. The implicit assumption in these regressions is that the regulatory monitoring variables are in part driven by a bank's performance, financial condition, macroeconomic factors, market factors, and bank-specific factors. Controlling for these other factors should help in isolating the impact of regulatory pressure on management turnover.

The primary specification results, based on the logistic regression described in equation (1), are reported in columns (1) and (2) of table 4.[21] The number of observations drops from over 74,000 in the univariate tests to about 59,000 in these multivariate regressions. This is because bank fixed effects are included and the logistic regression drops observations without any change in the turnover variable across time.[22] If the dropped observations constitute banks that are systematically different from those remaining, the coefficients may be biased. To explore whether this materially affects the results, variations of equations (1) and (2) are explored in columns (3)–(6). Columns (3) and (4) report the same results as in columns (1) and (2), respectively, based on a logistic regression without bank fixed effects; the last two columns present these results using a linear probability model with bank fixed effects.

Column (1) of table 4 reports the results of regressing turnover (EXTURN) on performance (ROA), financial controls (FC), and nonfinancial controls (NFC). The results suggest that poor performance (ROA) is strongly associated with executive turnover. Column (2) reports the same regression as in column (1) but includes the regulatory monitoring variables MANRAT, CHANGERAT, and EXAMINED. Each of the regulatory variables has a positive and significant coefficient suggesting that greater regulatory pressure is a driver of bank executive turnover. Also, the adjusted R-square increases in column (2) relative to column (1). The effect of regulatory monitoring appears economically significant as well.

---

[21] Because the logit specification has bank fixed effects, no constant term can be estimated.

[22] Without variation in the dependent variable, observations of a given bank will have either all positive or all negative outcomes and computation of a fixed effect becomes impossible for this procedure.

Results in column (2) indicate that having a poor managerial rating (MANRAT) increases the odds of executive turnover by e(0.25) = 1.28 and a ratings worsening (CHANGERAT) leads to an increase in turnover odds by e(0.14) = 1.14.[23] Finally, banks that have been examined recently also have higher turnover odds by e(0.13) = 1.14.

The results in column (2) also indicate that the poor performance (ROA) and higher PDUE90 are significantly associated with executive turnover and that CAPRAT and LIQUID are not. The coefficients of ROA and PDUE90, while diminishing somewhat from column (1), are still significant in the expected directions; this suggests that board discipline based on these variables is not replaced by regulatory oversight. The magnitude of the coefficient of CAPRAT, however, does drop down significantly from column (1). This drop suggests that regulatory oversight, besides focusing on private, nonfinancial information obtained in bank examinations, also considers poor risk management, as captured by low capital ratios. Taken together, the significance and direction of the coefficients of the performance and financial condition variables indicate that, after factoring in regulatory pressure, nonfinancial controls, bank fixed effects, and time fixed effects, bank boards of directors and shareholders consider performance (ROA) and to some extent credit risk (PDUE90) to be the primary metrics for judging bank executives' performance.[24]

Many of the other controls have significant relationships with turnover. The size variable, LGASSET, seems to be negatively related to turnover in most specifications and significant in many of these. One explanation could be that smaller banks are less stable and

---

[23] As an alternative to MANRAT, I also experiment with a dummy indicating a "good" versus "bad" rating (i.e., a rating of "1" or "2" versus a rating of "3," "4," or "5." I also estimate equation (1) while replacing MANRAT with dummies for each individual rating. The latter of these methods best addresses any potential nonlinear relationship between ratings and turnover. Tests using these alternative measures, not reported, lead to similar results.

[24] An alternative measure of performance to ROA is ROE (return on equity). Additional tests, not reported, indicate these results are robust to the use of ROE to measure performance.

more likely to be acquired; alternatively, because larger banks tend to be more profitable and better governed, they have less need for forced turnover. The change in size (CHLGASSET) variable is strongly and negatively related to turnover in all specifications; this may indicate bank owners punish bank management for poor growth.

The variable ACQUIRE is significantly and positively associated with executive turnover across all specifications; this is consistent with the explanation that firms undergoing merger activity have redundant executive positions and experience more turnover. The coefficient for DENOVO is positive and mostly significant across specifications, which indicates that newer banks tend to have more management turnover.

Unsurprisingly, banks with changes in ownership (OWNCHANGE) are found to be more likely to have turnover; this is likely because of redundant management or other organizational changes initiated by changes in ownership. The number of banks in the market (BANKSMKT), on the other hand, is not related to turnover in any specification; the percentage of other banks with turnover (EXTURNMKT) is strongly associated with more turnover. Lastly, short tenure (TENSHORT) is associated more executive turnover in all specifications.

Results from the logistic regression without fixed effects, reported in columns (3) and (4), and the linear probability model, reported in columns (4) and (5), generally confirm the results in columns (1) and (2). The degree of significance and relative impact of each variable varies, however. For example, the coefficient of EXAMINED is almost twice that of CHANGERATE in column (4), whereas the coefficient of EXAMINED is less than the coefficient of CHANGERATE in columns (2) and (6). This suggests that a model without fixed effects, while confirming the overall relationship of the primary specification, may result in biased coefficients because of the treatment of observations from the same bank as independent. The results based on the linear probability model, reported in columns (5) and (6), also must be interpreted with caution because of the well-known problems of estimating linear models with dummy dependent variables; still, estimates from this model can be seen as convenient approximations, because linear probability models generally give acceptable estimates for common values of the explanatory variables.[25]

Because of potential problems with estimating the effect of regulatory oversight and performance on turnover without bank fixed effects or with a linear probability model, the remaining analysis in this paper focuses on the results in columns (1) and (2). Still, the additional tests in columns (3)–(6) by and large confirm the results in columns (1) and (2) and are important in showing that the results from columns (1) and (2) do not depend on the exclusion of banks without turnover.[26] Overall, the results in table 4 are consistent with the explanation that both performance and regulatory oversight are factors in driving top management turnover in banks and that regulatory oversight serves to complement the role of board oversight.[27]

---

[25] The linear probability model is associated with heteroskedastic error terms, non-normally distributed errors, and predicted values that can be outside the range of (0, 1). A more complete explanation of the benefits and drawbacks of linear probability models is provided in Woodridge (2002, chapter 15).

[26] The multivariate tests, reported in table 4, were also estimated for each of the periods 1985–1988, 1989–1991, and 1992–1994. The results were similar in terms of directions of coefficients but weaker in terms of significance, especially in the latter two time periods, perhaps owing to not enough observations. Further multivariate tests using the subperiod 1989–1994 were similar in both direction and significance.

[27] The results, while finding strong associations between performance and turnover and regulatory oversight and turnover, do not definitively establish that performance and regulatory oversight cause turnover. For example, to the extent executive turnover is indicative of poor governance, turnover could also lead to poor performance and, given this possibility, the results should be taken with some caution. Still, given the use of lagged measures of performance and regulatory oversight, which greatly reduce the possibility of endogeneity and reverse causality in the findings, the results are consistent with performance and regulatory oversight driving turnover.

### c) Multivariate Tests: Future Profitability and Managerial Turnover

The results of univariate and multivariate tests relating managerial turnover to regulatory oversight suggest that regulatory oversight serves a complementary role to board discipline in the sense that both weak performance and greater regulatory pressure is related to increased likelihood of turnover. If regulatory-linked management turnover in banks is solely driven by compliance issues, however, this turnover may not prove directly beneficial to banks. On the other hand, if regulatory-linked turnover leads to improved governance, it should also lead to improved bank performance. To explore this issue, I next examine whether management turnover attributable to regulatory oversight is related to future bank performance.

These additional tests may also help evaluate whether the results from tests relating regulatory oversight to turnover were due to misspecification. The implicit assumption in these previous tests was that bank regulators pressure bank boards to fire their management primarily if inefficient or self-dealing tendencies in management are found; thus it is also implicit that regulatory-linked turnover is likely to improve bank performance. However, if the regressions relating executive turnover to regulatory oversight are misspecified, the positive association between EXTURN and the regulatory variables could be spurious. In particular, if EXTURN is not really driven by MANRAT, CHANGERAT, or EXAMINED and instead is driven by variables correlated with the regulatory variables, then the interpretation of these results would not be correct and management turnover induced by the regulatory variables should not be positively related to subsequent performance. Alternatively, if turnover linked to regulatory pressure is found to be positively related to future performance, then equation (1) is likely to be correctly specified.

23

To explore whether regulatory-linked turnover is beneficial to bank owners, I relate performance (ROA) to the predicted likelihood of executive turnover attributed to the regulatory variables. The predicted likelihood of executive turnover is estimated by means of the procedure used by Core et al. (1999), Bertrand and Mullainathan (2001), and others. This involves obtaining the predicted value of EXTURN from the regression of EXTURN on regulatory oversight, performance, and other controls, (i.e., the results based on equation (1) reported in column (2) of table 4). However, instead of estimating predicted values in the usual sense, I estimate the predicted value using only the regulatory variables. Thus EL_EXTURN ("excess" likelihood of executive turnover) is defined as:

$$(2) \quad Log(\frac{EL\_EXTURN_{i,t}}{1 - EL\_EXTURN_{i,t}}) = b_0 * MANRAT_{i,t-1} + b_1 * CHANGERAT_{i,t-1}$$
$$+ b_2 * RECENTEXAM_{i,t-1}$$

In equation (2), $b_0$, $b_1$, and $b_2$ are the estimated coefficients for MANRAT, CHANGERAT, and EXAMINED reported in table 4, column (2). After obtaining estimates for EL_EXTURN, I next execute regressions of performance on lagged EL_EXTURN and other controls.[28] EL_EXTURN$_{i,t-k}$ in equation (3) represents regulatory-linked turnover for bank i exactly k quarters in the past (k = 4, 8, 12, and 16 in columns (1), (2), (3), and (4), respectively); the results of these regressions are reported in table 5. As before, FC indicates the financial control variables PDUE90, CAPRAT, LIQUID, LGASSET, and CHLGASSET. I include lagged ROA on the right-hand side of equation (3) because past performance is a key indicator of future performance.

---

[28] To be consistent with the estimation equation (1), I only include banks that had at least one change in senior management during the entire observation period. Additional tests, not reported, indicate that the results for equation (3) do not depend on this data reduction.

$$ROA_{i,t} = Ø_0 * EL\_EXTURN_{i,t-k} + Ø_1 * ROA_{i,t-1} + \sum_{j=2}^{7} Ø_j * FC_{j;i,t-1} + TIME_t$$

(3)

$$+ BANK_i + \varepsilon_{i,t}$$

Because the regressions in columns (1), (2), (3), and (4) of table 5 require banks to survive for 4, 8, 12, or 16 quarters after the quarter of regulatory-linked turnover, there is the potential for substantial selection bias. For example, only banks that survive sixteen quarters (i.e., four years) past the quarter of regulatory-linked turnover are included in the regression indicated by column (4) of table 5. If banks that face regulatory-linked management turnover fail during this four-year period because of poor performance, then the effect of regulatory-linked turnover on performance will be overstated; alternatively, if these banks exit primarily because of superior performance (i.e., if better-performing banks are acquired), the effect of turnover attributable to regulatory pressure on performance will be understated.

In either case, the bias will be strongest in regressions with the four-year lag and less strong for the regressions with shorter lags. To minimize the impact of selection bias, the regressions reported in table 5 are re-estimated using a Heckman two-step procedure (Heckman, 1979) to control for the likelihood of surviving long enough to remain in the sample. The first step of the Heckman estimation, not reported, uses a probit model and estimates whether a bank survives over a given time period as a function of performance (ROA), the financial condition variables (FC) used in equations (1) and (3), market competition (BANKSMKT), and economic environment (TIME DUMMIES). A transformed version of the predicted probability of survival arising from the estimation, the inverse-mills ratio (INVERSEMILLS), is then added to the regression specified by equation (3). This is the second step of the procedure and is reported in table 5 columns (5)–(8) for regulatory-linked turnover one, two, three, and four years in the past, respectively.

25

The results in table 5 columns (1)–(4) and (5)–(8) indicate that turnover attributable to regulatory pressure (EL_EXTURN) is positively related to future ROA for each of four years following this turnover. The results are significant, but weakest, one year after regulatory-linked turnover. This is not unexpected because new management may need time to implement positive change.[29] The results appear weaker, but still significant, after factoring in the likelihood of firm survival (i.e., inclusion of INVERSEMILLS); the significance of the INVERSEMILLS ratio suggests that controlling for survival bias is important.

The estimated coefficients in columns (5)–(8) indicate that as the portion of executive turnover likelihood implied by regulatory actions (EL_EXTURN) increases from 0 to 1, ROA increases by 20, 37, 26, and 24 basis points in one, two, three, and four years, respectively. Alternatively, turnover attributable to a downgrade of one level (CHANGERAT = 1) that results in MANRAT going from a "1" to a "2" with an exam having been conducted in the last 18 months (EXAMINED = 1), is associated with an ROA higher by about 9 basis points in one year, 16 basis points in two years, 11 basis points in three years, and 10 basis points in four years. If MANRAT instead goes from "3" to "4" and CHANGERAT and EXAMINED are as above, then regulatory-linked turnover leads to a higher ROA in one, two, three, and four years of 11, 21, 15, and 13 basis points, respectively.[30]

In all columns of table 5, higher lagged ROA is associated with better future ROA, as might be expected, because past performance is an excellent predictor of future performance. In contrast, higher capital (CAPRAT) is associated with lower future ROA in all

---

[29] Robustness tests, using ROE to measure performance, were conducted. The results, not reported, were very similar.

[30] These estimates are calculated using equation (2) to first estimate the EL_EXTURN implied by MANRAT, CHANGERAT, and EXAMINED. The estimated value for EL_EXTURN is then applied to the estimated coefficient for EL_EXTURN in equation (3) to estimate the effect as described. For example, if a downgrade (CHANGERAT = 1) leading to a managerial rating of "3" (MANRAT = 3) leads to an increase in EL_EXTURN of X, the implied increase in ROA in one year is 0.0020 * X.

specifications. This may be because higher financial leverage (or lower capital ratios) may be indicative of poor financial condition only at very high levels. In general, a lower capital ratio may be indicative of higher risk, which implies a higher ROA.[31] Also, better liquidity (LIQUID) and lower past-due loans (PDUE90) are associated with better performance, as might be expected.

The regressions also indicate bank size (LGASSET) and change in size (CHLGASSET) affect future profitability. The LGASSET term is significantly and negatively related to future ROA in all specifications. A possible cause of any negative relationship between bank size and future profitability is that larger firms, although possibly enjoying economies of scale, may be less efficient than smaller firms. The results also indicate that ROA tends to be higher in growing firms (higher CHLGASSET); the results for this variable are significant in all columns.

## IV. Sensitivity/Robustness Tests

### a) Timing of Regulatory Interventions

Equation (1) assumes that MANRAT implicitly factors in the effect of past downgrades and thus the CHANGERAT variable is included only for the most recent lagged quarter. To the extent downgrades at other time lags are important in explaining turnover, the results in table 4 could be biased. To explore this possibility, I experiment with including lagged rating changes six quarters in the past. Though the coefficients of some of the earlier lags (i.e., second, third, and fourth quarters) are somewhat significant, the inclusion of these variables dramatically reduces the coefficients of the supervisory rating variable, MANRAT,

---

[31] Traditional corporate financial theory suggests a risk-return tradeoff. That is, investors must be compensated for higher risk by receiving a higher expected return.

and does not lead to an improvement in the overall R-square of the regression. These additional tests suggest that the supervisory rating, MANRAT, already largely incorporates the effect of past downgrades beyond one quarter and the inclusion of the variable indicating downgrade in the most recent quarter along with the managerial rating leads to an appropriate specification.[32]

Another issue is whether bank regulators really provide new information to the board or simply confirm a board's findings by downgrading a bank's management ratings when poor governance or other evidence of ineffective management is found. If a bank's board observes the same things bank regulators do and acts on these independently of regulatory actions, then the regulatory variables may be correlated with unobserved board variables and the board variables may really be driving executive turnover. The inclusion of bank fixed effects in equation (1) and the use of lagged indicators of regulatory pressure greatly reduce the likelihood of this possibility. To explore the issue further, I examine bank executive turnover in relation to the timing of regulatory downgrades of management ratings. If management turnover is driven by supervisory oversight and not by board variables correlated with this oversight, then turnover should occur more frequently in the quarter after a ratings downgrade than in the quarter before. Additional tests, not reported, suggest that rating downgrades are much more likely to be associated with executive turnover when the downgrade occurs in the quarter prior to turnover, relative to the quarter after turnover. This suggests that regulatory oversight, as opposed to unobserved board variables, is driving executive turnover in banks.

---

[32] I also experiment with a "time-to-ruin" model, where the time to a turnover event is related to past downgrade events. The results suggest that downgrades are related to a reduced time to turnover for the first three quarter lags, but that the effect is much more significant in the quarter immediately prior to the turnover. As before, the inclusion of lagged CHANGERAT more than one quarter in the past significantly diminishes the coefficient of MANRAT.

### b) Direct Impact of Regulatory Intervention and Performance

Bank examinations may lead to improved bank performance independent of executive turnover. But, because management is more likely to leave poorly performing and poorly rated banks, the results in table 5 might represent a spurious correlation between regulatory-linked turnover and performance. To examine this possibility, the results in table 5 were re-estimated while replacing EL_EXTURN (regulatory-linked turnover) with the ratings and downgrade variables directly. The results suggest that past downgrades, in general, are associated with *worse* performance and recent exams have no discernable effect on performance. The effect of past management ratings on performance is positive but small in magnitude. Overall, the additional test results suggest that it is more the regulatory-linked turnover, and not as much the direct impact of regulatory oversight, that leads to better subsequent performance.

### c) Impact of "Forced" Dismissals

In some cases, bank regulators order banks to remove executives. To the extent that these orders are given in conjunction with a ratings downgrade, the relation between the departure of an executive and the downgrade would be spurious. Because regulator-ordered removals of executives are rare events, this is unlikely to affect the results. In cases when executives are ordered to be dismissed, the orders are typically associated with formal regulatory actions. To examine whether the effect of formal actions alter the results, an additional variable was added to equation (1) indicating that a formal action occurred in the quarter. The inclusion of this variable did not materially affect the results.[33]

### d) Omitted Observations

The regression described by equation (1) measures performance using ROA and to some extent PDUE90, LIQUID, and CAPRAT. To the extent other measures of performance are excluded, the results could be biased. One important measure of performance is bank survival, especially because bank failure can be the ultimate failure of bank governance. Because failed banks fall out of the sample, regression (1) implicitly excludes the effect of bank failure. This problem is minimized in part because banks that fail will have low levels of financial performance as captured as ROA, PDUE90, LIQUID, and CAPRAT and the inclusion of these variables helps to capture the impact of potential failure. As an additional test, equation (1) was re-estimated while excluding banks that failed during the sample. The results, not reported, were qualitatively similar to those reported in table 4.

### e) Reversals

A central theme of this paper is that regulatory-linked management changes are associated with better bank governance. As an additional test of this central theme, I explore the issue of whether turnover attributable to regulatory oversight is associated with future regulatory upgrades. Such a reversal effect, to the extent it is observed, adds weight to the argument that regulatory-linked turnover leads to better bank governance. A simple correlation analysis, not reported, indicates that regulatory-linked turnover (EL_EXTURN) in

---

[33] In these tests, a formal action is defined as a "cease and desist order," a "civil money penalty," a "prompt corrective action," a "formal agreement," or a "removal or prohibition order."

the past is strongly related to upgrades in the future; this suggests that subsequent ratings upgrades are not independent of regulatory-induced turnover and that there is a reversal effect.

## V. Conclusions

This paper has provided evidence that both weak performance and regulatory monitoring are related to greater executive turnover in banks; the results suggest that regulatory evaluations of management serve to complement the role of board oversight. Further, the evidence is consistent with the explanation that regulatory-driven executive turnover is beneficial for banks in that it leads to improved subsequent performance. Finally, because this paper utilizes a unique sample of predominantly small and private banks, the results imply that neither board oversight nor regulatory oversight depend on the market pressures of publicly traded firms.

The results also add to the growing body of evidence that regulatory oversight, more generally, can be effective as a monitoring mechanism. The results may be especially relevant in the context of the current debate on reforming financial regulation. Although the results do not imply that all forms of financial regulation are beneficial in all contexts, they do imply that regulatory oversight focused on improving governance can be valuable.

## VI. References

Barro, J., and R. Barro. "Pay, Performance, and Turnover of Bank CEOs." *Journal of Labor Economics*, 8 (1991), 448–481.

Bertrand, M., and S. Mullainathan. "Are CEOs Rewarded for Luck? The Ones Without Principals Are." *Quarterly Journal of Economics,* 116 (2001), 901–932.

Brickley, J.A. "Empirical Research on CEO Turnover and Firm-Performance: A Discussion." *Journal of Accounting and Economics*, 36 (2003), 227–233.

Borokovich, K., Parrino, R., and T. Trapani. "Outside Directors and CEO Selection." *Journal of Financial and Quantitative Analysis*, 31 (1996), 337–354.

Canella, A., Fraser, D., and S. Lee. "Firm Failure and Managerial Labor Markets: Evidence from Texas Banking." *Journal of Financial Economics,* 38 (1995), 185–210.

Core, J., Holthausen, R., and P. Kumar. "Corporate Governance, Chief Executive Compensation, and Firm Performance." *Journal of Financial Economics,* 51 (1999), 371–406.

Cook, D., Hogan, A., and R. Kieschnick. "A Study of the Corporate Governance of Thrifts." *Journal of Banking and Finance*, 28 (2004), 1247–1271.

Crespi, R., Garcia-Cestona, M., and V. Salas. "Governance Mechanisms in Spanish Banks. Does Ownership Matter?" *Journal of Banking and Finance,* 28 (2004), 2311–2330.

Dahl, D., O'Keefe, J., and G. Hanweck. "The Influence of Examiners and Auditors on Loan-Loss Recognition." *FDIC Banking Review,* 11 (1998), 10–25.

Dahya, J., McConnell, J.J., and N. G. Travlos. "The Cadbury Committee, Corporate Performance, and Top Management Turnover." *Journal of Finance*, 57 (2002), 461–483.

Denis, D., and D.K. Denis. "Performance Changes Following Top Management Dismissals." *Journal of Finance*, 50 (1995), 1029–1058.

DeYoung, R., Flannery, M., Lang, W., and and S. Sorescu. "The Information Content of Bank Examination Ratings and Subordinated Debt Prices." *Journal of Money Credit and Banking*, 33 (1998), 900–925.

Fabozzi, F., Modigliani, F., Jones, F.J., and M.G. Ferri. "The Role of Government in Financial Markets." In *Foundations of Financial Markets and Institutions*, 3rd edition, Saddle River, NJ, (2002).

Farrell, G. "Under fire, Merrill Lynch CEO O'Neal retires." *USA TODAY* Online Edition, October, (2007).

Finfacts Team. "US Home Depot CEO Nardelli fired with golden boot worth $210 million." *Finfacts Ireland, Business & Finance Portal* (www.finfacts.ie), (2007).

Fiseman, R., Khurana, R., and Rhodes-Kropf, M. "Governance and CEO Turnover: Do Something or Do the Right Thing." Harvard Business School Working Paper, (2005).

Frater, S., and M. Pollick. "Bradenton's Coast Bank Ordered to Fire its CEO." *Herald Tribune* Online Edition, (2007).

Gardner, S. "Westsound CEO to Resign." *Kitsap Sun* Online Edition, (2008).

Heckman, J. "Sample Selection Bias as a Specification Error." *Econometrica*, 47 (1979) 153–161.

Gibson, M. "Is Corporate Governance Ineffective in Emerging Markets." *Journal of Financial and Quantitative Analysis*, 38 (2003), 231–250.

Gunther, J., and R. Moore. "Loss Underreporting and the Auditing Role of Bank Exams." *Journal of Financial Intermediation*, 12 (2003), 153–177.

Houston, J., and C. James. "Management and Organizational Changes in Banking: A Comparison of Regulatory Intervention with Private Creditor Actions in Non-Bank Firms." *Carnegie-Rochester Conference Series on Public Policy*, 38 (1993), 143–178.

Hotchkiss, E.S. "Postbankruptcy Performance and Management Turnover." *Journal of Finance*, 50 (1995), 3–21.

Huson, M.R., Parrino, R., and L.T. Starks. "Internal Monitoring Mechanisms and CEO Turnover: A Long-Term Perspective." *Journal of Finance*, 56 (2001) 2265–2297.

Ionnatta, G. "Testing for Opaqueness in the European Banking Industry: Evidence from Bond Credit Ratings." SDS Boccon Working Paper, (2004).

Karpoff, J.M., Lee, D.S., and G.S. Martin. "The Consequences to Managers for Financial Misrepresentation." *Journal of Financial Economics*, (2008).

Khorana, A. "Performance Changes Following Top Management Turover: Evidence from Open-Ended Mutual Funds." *Journal of Financial and Quantitative Analysis*, 36 (2001), 371–393.

Morgan, D. "Rating Banks: Risk and Uncertainty in an Opaque Industry." *American Economic Review*, 92 (2002), 874–888.

Office of the Comptroller of Currency. "Outsourcing Your Audit Function," 2002, (transcript of presentation by J.D. Hawke, Jr., Z. Blackburn, M. Blair, C.S. Schainost, R.T. Riordan, and W.E. Baker).

Peek, J., Rosengren, E., and G. Tootell. "Does the Federal Reserve Have an Informational Advantage? You Can Bet On It." Federal Reserve Bank of Boston Working Paper, (1998).

Prowse, S. "Alternative Methods of Corporate Control in Commercial Banks." *Economic Review*, Federal Reserve Bank of Dallas Working Paper, (1995).

Reeves, S. "Brystol-Myers CEO Quits," *Forbes.com*, (2006).

Webb, E. "Regulator scrutiny and bank CEO incentives." *Journal of Financial Services Research,* 33, (2008), 5–20.

Weisbach, M. "Outside Directors and CEO Turnover." *Journal of Financial Economics*, 20 (1988), 431–460.

Wheelock, D., and P. Wilson. "Why Do Banks Disappear: The Determinants of U.S. Bank Failures and Acquisitions." Federal Reserve Bank of St. Louis Working Paper, (1995).

Woodridge, J. "Discrete Response Models." In *Econometric Analysis of Cross Section and Panel Data*, Massachusetts Institute of Technology, Cambridge, MA, (2002).

## Table 1. Variable Names, Definitions, and Summary Statistics

Summary statistics detailed in this table are primarily based on quarterly call report data from 1985 to 1994. Regulatory variables are derived from data obtained from the Office of Comptroller of the Currency. The variable CHANGERAT is summarized only for bank observations when there was a change in the rating (about 7.4 percent of observations); this is done to present a meaningful distribution of ratings changes. Finally, all financial variables are winsorized to the bottom and top 1 percent values. LGASSET and CHLGASSET reflect assets measured in thousands of dollars.

| Variable Name and Defintinion | Number of Obs | Mean | Percentiles | | | | |
| --- | --- | --- | --- | --- | --- | --- | --- |
| | | | 5th | 25th | 50th | 75th | 95th |
| EXTURN<br>*Indicates senior officer change* | 73269 | 8.51% | 0.00% | 0.00% | 0.00% | 0.00% | 100.00% |
| MANRAT<br>*Supervisory rating (i.e. 1,2,3,4, or 5)* | 73269 | 2.33 | 1.00 | 2.00 | 2.00 | 3.00 | 4.00 |
| CHANGERAT<br>*Indicates change in MANRAT* | 5420 | 0.06 | -1.00 | -1.00 | 1.00 | 1.00 | 2.00 |
| EXAMINED<br>*Indicates exam occurred in last 18 months* | 73269 | 88.46% | 0.00% | 100.00% | 100.00% | 100.00% | 100.00% |
| LGASSET<br>*Log of assets* | 73269 | 10.48 | 9.30 | 10.03 | 10.54 | 10.98 | 11.43 |
| CHLGASSET<br>*Change in log assets (since last quarter)* | 73269 | 0.07 | -0.09 | 0.00 | 0.05 | 0.11 | 0.30 |
| CAPRAT<br>*(Tier 1) Capital ratio* | 73269 | 9.24% | 4.98% | 7.23% | 8.66% | 10.62% | 15.36% |
| ROA<br>*Return on assets* | 73269 | 0.77% | -1.48% | 0.55% | 0.99% | 1.36% | 2.02% |
| PDUE90<br>*Loans 90 days past due to assets* | 73269 | 1.27% | 0.01% | 0.28% | 0.79% | 1.69% | 4.36% |
| LIQUID<br>*Non-volatile Liabilities to assets* | 73269 | 88.67% | 70.92% | 84.60% | 90.86% | 95.04% | 98.55% |
| DENOVO<br>*Indicates new bank (5 or fewer years)* | 73269 | 11.58% | 0.00% | 0.00% | 0.00% | 0.00% | 100.00% |
| ACQUIRE<br>*Indicates acquired another bank* | 73269 | 0.53% | 0.00% | 0.00% | 0.00% | 0.00% | 0.00% |
| OWNCHANGE<br>*Indicates change in bank ownership* | 73269 | 1.01% | 0.00% | 0.00% | 0.00% | 0.00% | 0.00% |
| BANKSMKT<br>*Number of banks in market* | 73269 | 35.34 | 2.00 | 4.00 | 7.00 | 26.00 | 170.00 |
| EXTURNMKT<br>*% of other banks in market with turnover* | 73269 | 8.10% | 0.00% | 0.00% | 0.00% | 13.30% | 31.45% |

## Table 2. Regulatory Oversight and Performance: Univariate Tests

In the table below, results of univariate tests examining the effect of performance and regulatory oversight on top management turnover are presented. Tests of differences are done using standard unpaired t-tests. Test significance is denoted by *** (p-value < 0.01), ** (p-value between 0.05 and 0.01), and * (p-value between 0.1 and 0.05). The variables MANRAT and CHANGERAT indicate regulatory ratings of bank management and changes in management ratings, respectively. EXAMINED indicates an exam occurred in the previous 18 months. ROA refers to return on assets.

| Time Period | Variable | No Executive Changes | At least 1 Executive Change | No Change vs Change |
|---|---|---|---|---|
| | | (N= 30,497) | (N= 3,245) | |
| 1985-1988 | ROA | 0.72% | -0.02% | *** |
| | MANRAT | 2.26 | 2.64 | *** |
| | CHANGERATE | 0.01 | 0.08 | *** |
| | EXAMINED | 80.15% | 89.46% | *** |
| | | (N= 19,463) | (N= 1,763) | |
| 1989-1991 | ROA | 0.79% | 0.16% | *** |
| | MANRAT | 2.33 | 2.72 | *** |
| | CHANGERATE | 0.01 | 0.06 | |
| | EXAMINED | 93.62% | 94.84% | *** |
| | | (N= 17,071) | (N= 1,230) | |
| 1992-1994 | ROA | 1.06% | 0.64% | *** |
| | MANRAT | 2.31 | 2.72 | *** |
| | CHANGERATE | -0.03 | 0.01 | *** |
| | EXAMINED | 95.89% | 97.89% | *** |

## Table 3. Simultaneous Effect of Regulatory Oversight and Performance: Univariate Tests

This table describes univariate tests that simultaneously examine the effects of regulatory oversight and performance on management turnover. Quartiles of ROA (return on assets) are taken for each time period.. Tests of differences are done using standard unpaired t-tests. Test significance is denoted by *** (p-value < 0.01), ** (p-value between 0.05 and 0.01), and * (p-value between 0.1 and 0.05). The variable MANRAT represents regulatory ratings of bank management and CHANGERAT indicates changes in MANRAT. EXAMINED indicates an exam occurred in the previous 18 months.

| ROA Quartile | Variable | No Executive Changes | At least 1 Executive Change | No Change vs Change |
|---|---|---|---|---|
| | | (N= 15,252) | (N= 2,803) | |
| ROA - Quartile 1 | MANRAT | 2.75 | 3.04 | *** |
| (Lowest) | CHANGERAT | 0.04 | 0.12 | *** |
| | EXAMINED | 0.94 | 0.95 | *** |
| | | (N= 16,812) | (N= 1,444) | |
| ROA - Quartile 2 | MANRAT | 2.29 | 2.48 | *** |
| | CHANGERAT | 0.00 | 0.01 | * |
| | EXAMINED | 0.90 | 0.93 | *** |
| | | (N= 17,461) | (N= 1,039) | |
| ROA - Quartile 3 | MANRAT | 2.12 | 2.28 | *** |
| | CHANGERAT | -0.01 | 0.00 | * |
| | EXAMINED | 0.86 | 0.89 | *** |
| | | (N= 17,506) | (N= 952) | |
| ROA - Quartile 4 | MANRAT | 2.07 | 2.32 | *** |
| (Highest) | CHANGERAT | -0.02 | 0.01 | *** |
| | EXAMINED | 0.82 | 0.89 | *** |

## Table 4. Determinants of Executive Turnover: Multivariate Tests

The dependent variable, in each of the regressions summarized in this table, is EXTURN (executive turnover in the current quarter). Regulatory oversight, performance, and financial condition regressors are lagged. Columns (1)–(4) represent logistic regression results; columns (5) and (6) present linear probability model results. The reported R-squares represent adjusted R-squares for the linear probability models and pseudo R-squares for the logistic regressions. Similarly, overall regression p-values are for F-tests and chi-square tests for the linear probability models and logistic models, respectively. T-stats are presented in parentheses below the each regression coefficient. The asterisks indicate significance of the regression coefficients. Significance at the 1-percent level is indicated by ***. Similarly ** and * indicate significance at the 5-percent and 10-percent levels, respectively. The variables MANRAT and CHANGERAT indicate regulatory ratings of bank management and changes in these ratings, respectively. EXAMINED indicates an exam occurred in the previous 18 months. ROA, PDUE90, CAPRAT, and LIQUID represent return on assets, loans 90 days past due to assets, and ratio of nonvolatile to volatile assets, respectively. LGASSET and CHLGASSET represent log of assets and change in log of assets. DENOVO indicates a bank chartered within the last five years. ACQUIRE indicates that a bank has acquired another bank and CHANGEOWN indicates a change in bank affiliation. BNKSMKT indicates the number of banks in the metropolitan statistical area or rural county. EXTURNMKT indicates the percentage of banks with turnover in the quarter and TENSHORT indicates short tenure, i.e., executive turnover in the last quarter.

| | (1) | (2) | (3) | (4) | (5) | (6) |
|---|---|---|---|---|---|---|
| MANRAT | | 0.2527 *** | | 0.2846 *** | | 0.0219 *** |
| | | (9.77) | | (13.93) | | (9.26) |
| CHANGERAT | | 0.1365 *** | | 0.1188 *** | | 0.0168 *** |
| | | (3.58) | | (3.01) | | (4.11) |
| EXAMINED | | 0.1280 ** | | 0.1924 *** | | 0.0057 * |
| | | (2.15) | | (3.62) | | (1.79) |
| ROA | -11.9272 *** | -8.9338 *** | -15.0209 *** | -11.3523 *** | -1.5705 *** | -1.2729 *** |
| | -(9.10) | -(6.67) | -(13.08) | -(9.74) | -(9 56) | -(7.69) |
| PDUE90 | 7.3103 *** | 4.6546 *** | 8 2877 *** | 3.5639 *** | 0.7715 *** | 0.5173 *** |
| | (6.03) | (3.74) | (8.99) | (3.65) | (5.82) | (3.84) |
| CAPRAT | -1.6632 ** | 0.0228 | -2.6545 *** | -1.0192 ** | -0.1624 * | -0.0195 |
| | -(2.05) | (0.03) | -(5.62) | -(2.19) | -(1 91) | -(0.23) |
| LIQUID | 0.0875 | -0.0291 | -0.6068 *** | -0.5136 *** | -0.0010 | -0.0084 |
| | (0.26) | -(0.09) | -(3.61) | -(3.06) | -(0.03) | -(0.26) |
| LGASSET | -0.1931 ** | -0.1033 | -0.1136 *** | -0.0605 *** | -0.0200 ** | -0.0134 |
| | -(2.26) | -(1.19) | -(5.09) | -(2.67) | -(2.44) | -(1.63) |
| CHLGASSET | -(0.81) *** | -(0.63) *** | -(0.72) *** | -(0.53) ** | -(0.09) *** | -(0.08) *** |
| | -(4.08) | -(3.17) | -(2.93) | -(2.19) | -(3.72) | -(3.20) |
| DENOVO | 0.1185 * | 0.1287 * | 0 2644 *** | 0.2877 *** | 0.0164 ** | 0.0165 ** |
| | (1.80) | (1.95) | (5.77) | (6.28) | (2 39) | (2.41) |
| ACQUIRE | 0.7088 *** | 0.6823 *** | 0.7766 *** | 0.7703 *** | 0.0627 *** | 0.0604 *** |
| | (4.08) | (3.91) | (4.80) | (4.72) | (3.70) | (3.56) |
| CHANGEOWN | 0.4865 *** | 0.5044 *** | 0.6255 *** | 0.6564 *** | 0.0445 *** | 0.0456 *** |
| | (4.06) | (4.21) | (5.53) | (5.79) | (3.63) | (3.72) |
| BANKSMKT | 0.0001 | 0.0004 | 0.0012 *** | 0.0011 *** | 0.0001 | 0.0001 |
| | (0.09) | (0.50) | (6.48) | (6.42) | (0.66) | (0.98) |
| EXURNMKT | 1.9632 *** | 1.9542 *** | 1.8435 *** | 1.8286 *** | 0.1760 *** | 0.1751 *** |
| | (21.63) | (21.45) | (25.09) | (24.71) | (17.71) | (17.67) |
| TENSHORT | 0.3752 *** | 0.3450 *** | 1.0380 *** | 0.9846 *** | 0.0540 *** | 0.0513 *** |
| | (10.27) | (9.39) | (28.23) | (26.43) | (10.09) | (9.57) |
| Constant Term | | | -0.7087 ** | -2.2553 *** | 0.3041 *** | 0.1770 * |
| | | | -(2.27) | -(6.83) | (3.15) | (1.81) |
| BANK FIXED EFFECTS | + | + | | | + | + |
| TIME FIXED EFFECTS | + | + | + | + | + | + |
| Number of Observations | 58155 | 58155 | 73272 | 73272 | 73272 | 73272 |
| Adjusted/Pseudo R-Square | 3.55% | 4.07% | 7.67% | 8.35% | 1.98% | 2.25% |
| F-Statistic/Chi-Square P-Value | 0.00 | 0.00 | 0.00 | 0.00 | 0.00 | 0.00 |

# Table 5. Future Profitability and Regulatory-Linked Turnover: Multivariate Tests

This table presents multivariate tests of the effect of regulatory-linked turnover (EL_EXTURN) on future profitability. EL_EXTURN is calculated based on equation (2) and the estimated coefficients in table 4, column (2). The dependent variable is ROA in each column. Columns (1)–(4) utilize values for EL_EXTURN (the portion of the likelihood of executive turnover explained only by the regulatory variables) 4, 8, 12, and 16 quarters ago, respectively. All other regressors represent values in the prior quarter. Columns (5)–(8) report the same results as columns (1)–(4) while utilizing a Heckman-type selection procedure to minimize the impact of firms without enough of history to compute the effect of lagged EL_EXTURN on profitability; the reported inverse-mills ratio (INVERSE MILLS) in these columns is a measure of the likelihood of firm survival. T-statistic significance at the 1-percent level is indicated by ***. Similarly ** and * indicate significance at the 5-percent and 10-percent levels, respectively. The variables LGASSET and CHLGASSET represent the log of assets and change in log of assets. ROA, PDUE90, CAPRAT, and LIQUID represent return on assets, loans 90 days past due to assets, and ration of nonvolatile to volatile assets, respectively.

| | (1) | (2) | (3) | (4) | (5) | (6) | (7) | (8) |
|---|---|---|---|---|---|---|---|---|
| EL_EXTURN (4 Qtrs Ago) | 0.0026 *** (3.25) | | | | 0.0020 ** (2.40) | | | |
| EL_EXTURN (8 Qtrs Ago) | | 0.0057 *** (7.67) | | | | 0.0037 *** (4.84) | | |
| EL_EXTURN (12 Qtrs Ago) | | | 0.0038 *** (5.51) | | | | 0.0026 *** (3.71) | |
| EL_EXTURN (16 Qtrs Ago) | | | | 0.0033 *** (5.21) | | | | 0.0024 *** (3.64) |
| LGASSET | -0.0007 *** (-3.74) | -0.0003 ** (-2.05) | -0.0005 *** (-3.34) | -0.0004 *** (-3.08) | -0.0006 *** (-3.12) | -0.0001 (-0.54) | -0.0003 ** (-2.29) | -0.0003 ** (-2.19) |
| CHLGASSET | 0.0027 *** (6.77) | 0.0018 *** (5.39) | 0.0020 *** (5.78) | 0.0009 *** (3.01) | 0.0026 *** (6.64) | 0.0017 *** (4.97) | 0.0019 *** (5.54) | 0.0008 *** (2.77) |
| CAPRAT | -0.0269 *** (-13.13) | -0.0191 *** (-9.57) | -0.0131 *** (-6.82) | -0.0081 *** (-4.52) | -0.0228 *** (-10.33) | -0.0143 *** (-6.97) | -0.0109 *** (-5.60) | -0.0070 *** (-3.84) |
| PDUE90 | -0.1311 *** (-43.09) | -0.1115 *** (-37.10) | -0.0963 *** (-32.13) | -0.0799 *** (-26.97) | -0.1315 *** (-43.22) | -0.1134 *** (-37.68) | -0.0964 *** (-32.18) | -0.0793 *** (-26.73) |
| ROA | 0.5982 *** (173.00) | 0.6092 *** (173.54) | 0.6195 *** (172.29) | 0.6257 *** (172.33) | 0.5968 *** (172.14) | 0.6063 *** (172.21) | 0.6174 *** (171.10) | 0.6247 *** (171.89) |
| LIQUID | 0.0088 *** (11.70) | 0.0077 *** (10.50) | 0.0063 *** (8.94) | 0.0054 *** (7.99) | 0.0085 *** (11.27) | 0.0076 *** (10.38) | 0.0064 *** (8.99) | 0.0054 *** (8.01) |
| INVERSE MILLS | | | | | 0.0133 *** (5.04) | 0.0069 *** (9.41) | 0.0031 *** (6.21) | 0.0022 *** (5.59) |
| CONSTANT TERM | 0.0041 * (1.86) | -0.0015 (-0.76) | 0.0021 (1.19) | 0.0022 (1.39) | 0.0032 (1.46) | -0.0035 * (-1.79) | 0.0007 (0.38) | 0.0011 (0.67) |
| BANK FIXED EFFECTS | + | + | + | + | + | + | + | + |
| TIME FIXED EFFECTS | + | + | + | + | + | + | + | + |
| Number of Observations | 58124 | 55470 | 52776 | 50145 | 58124 | 55470 | 52776 | 50145 |
| Adjusted R-Square | 44.26% | 44.86% | 44.32% | 44.53% | 44.28% | 44.95% | 44.36% | 44.57% |
| F-Statistic P-Value | 0.00 | 0.00 | 0.00 | 0.00 | 0.00 | 0.00 | 0.00 | 0.00 |